DECORATIVE CAKES

TESCO

ACKNOWLEDGEMENTS

The publishers would like to thank the following companies
for their kindness in providing materials and equipment
used in the photography for this book.

David Mellor, 4 Sloane Square, London SW1;
Elizabeth David, 46 Bourne Street, London SW1.

We would also like to thank the following who
were concerned in the preparation of the book.

Series Art Director Pedro Prá Lopez
Editor Mary Cadogan
Recipes on pages 36-7, 40, 42-3 devised by Stella Hartwell
Recipes for Space shuttle cake and Computer cake devised by Janice Murfitt
Photographer Paul Bussell (Martin Brigdale pages 45, 58)
Food prepared for photography by Mary Cadogan 25, 35, 50-53
Allyson Birch pages 45, 58
Carol Handslip pages 21, 23, 26-7, 41, 57,
Janice Murfitt pages 30-31, 33, 36-7, 38, 40, 42-3, 46-7, 48, 54-5, 59, 60-63
Rosemary Wadey page 29

CONTENTS

NOTE

Standard spoon measurements are used in all recipes

1 tablespoon (tbls) = one 15 ml spoon
1 teaspoon (tsp) = one 5 ml spoon
All spoon measures are level

All eggs are sizes 3 or 4 (standard) unless otherwise stated.

For all recipes, quantities are given in both
metric and imperial measures. Follow either set
but not a mixture of both, as they are not interchangeable.

W e set up our Consumer Advisory Service in response to the many pleas for information and cooking ideas we received from our customers. It is run by our team of qualified home economists who answer queries, offer practical advice on cookery and the home and give talks and demonstrations on new products and equipment.
The resounding success of the service and the continued demand for more and more recipes and information has now prompted us to produce our own special range of Tesco Cookery Books.
Our series starts with 12 books, each one focusing on an area that our customers have shown particular interest in. Each book contains practical background information on the chosen subject and concentrates on a wide selection of carefully tested recipes, each one illustrated in colour.

Most of us have wanted to make and decorate a cake at one time or another, but have been put off because it seemed so complicated. With *Decorative Cakes* to help, this need not happen, for all of the recipes are clearly and simply set out using diagrams and illustrated steps to guide wherever possible. Variety is the keynote: you'll find everything here from snowmen to tugboats, racing cars to valentines – not forgetting, of course, everyone's favourites for Christmas, Easter, christenings and weddings.
I very much hope you will enjoy looking through the pages which follow, trying out the recipes and above all tasting and enjoying the results. Happy Cooking!

Carey Dennis, senior home economist, Tesco Stores Ltd.

INTRODUCTION

Everybody loves special occasion, party and novelty cakes and these cakes can be great fun to make as well as to eat. In addition to the pleasures and rewards of home baking they provide scope for your own flair and invention in creating delightful cakes for every occasion. This book is full of ideas to help you develop these skills – from simple sponge cakes with a variety of finishes, fun birthday cakes you can make in an afternoon, to more elaborate novelty cakes and decorated rich fruit cakes for weddings and christenings.

Formal cake icing is a craft and as you practise it you will gain the confidence to try more intricate decorative finishes. The recipes in this book give clear and comprehensive instructions to guide you through every stage. We have also included a selection of basic recipes for mixtures, so you can be sure your cakes will taste every bit as good as they look.

Having the right equipment gives you a good start and we have included advice on buying tins, piping nozzles and other equipment you will need or may want to acquire. Special skills such as moulding leaves and flowers and piping roses are shown in clear step-by-step photographs. Give yourself plenty of time to practise before piping designs or lettering on the cake. Remember that cake decorating can be just as rewarding for the beginner as it is for the expert, and only practice makes perfect. You can have plenty of fun learning, and the results will give great pleasure to family and friends.

EQUIPMENT

Most of the cakes in this book can be made with the minimum of specialist equipment, but whatever you buy it is worthwhile choosing tins and utensils of good quality which will give you years of service. Most of the equipment you will need is now available in large department stores, supermarkets, kitchen shops, hardware stores or by post from cake decorating schools. The basic equipment which you will probably already have to hand should include the items listed in the box on the right. Try to keep a set of wooden spoons – perhaps two or three – purely for use in cake preparation. Always use nylon rather than metal sieves in cakemaking, to avoid any danger of flour or icing sugar becoming tainted when sieved. A rubber rather than wooden spatula is best for scraping cake mixture from the side of a mixing bowl.

A selection of bowls in various sizes
600 ml (1 pint) measuring jug
tablespoons and teaspoons
nylon sieves
wooden spoons
spatula
pastry brush
kitchen scissors
palette knife
small palette knife
or round-ended knife
skewers
string
rolling pin
small plastic containers with lids
supply of greaseproof, waxed
and non-stick paper
foil
icing nozzles (see page 16)
piping bag to fit larger nozzles

Other equipment which you may like to acquire as your interest and skills grow include the following:

> icing turntable
> icing nails
> icing comb or scraper
> metal or plastic templates
> 1 cup ruler
> cake markers
> fine paint brushes

Choosing Cake Tins

Buy good quality cake tins made from firm metal – these will keep their shape over years of use. Loose-based or springform tins are useful for removing cakes such as whisked sponges and victoria sponge mixtures which are easily damaged. When buying cake tins check their size by measuring across the base. The following provide a useful selection of sizes for most needs:

18 cm and 20 cm (7 and 8 inch) round deep cake tins
18 cm and 20 cm (7 and 8 inch) sandwich cake tins (two of each)
12 hole bun tray
18 cm x 28 cm (7 × 11 inch) shallow tin
23 cm × 33 cm (9 × 13 inch) shallow tin
20 cm (8 inch) square deep cake tin
23 cm (9 inch) diameter ring tin

As you progress with your cake making you may like to aim to have a set of tins, both round and square, which graduate in size. Other shapes of tin such as a heart, hexagon, horseshoe and numerals are worth collecting for special occasion cakes, and again these are available in a range of sizes. If they are not available from your usual supplier, cake decorating schools usually have a wide range available by post.

How to line cake tins

Tins will usually need to be greased and floured or greased and lined with non-stick or greaseproof paper. Melted lard or margarine are best for greasing tins, although oil can also be used. If you are using non-stick tins follow the manufacturer's instructions when preparing them for baking.

Lining the base of a round or square tin

This method is used for Victoria sandwich cakes, whisked sponges and light fruit cakes.
1. Place the base of the tin on a single sheet of greaseproof or non-stick paper, draw round the base with a pencil.
2. Cut out the paper along marked line.
3. Grease the inside of the tin, place the paper in the base and grease the paper.

To double line a deep round or square cake tin

Rich fruit cakes which require long cooking will need to be double lined with paper. As an extra precaution for very rich cakes it is a good idea to tie

● A selection of cake tins and boards that you will find useful in making many of the cakes that follow

double thickness brown paper around the outside of the cake tin to prevent the outside of the cake over-browning during baking.
1. Cut a strip of double thickness non-stick or greaseproof paper long enough to wrap around the outside of the tin with a small overlap, and wide enough to come 2.5 cm (1 inch) above rim of tin. Fold the bottom edge up 2 cm (¾ inch) and firmly mark a crease along the fold with your thumbnail.
2. Open out the crease and make slanting cuts up to the crease at 2.5 cm (1 inch) intervals.
3. Place the tin on a double thickness of paper and draw round the base. Cut around the marked line with a pair of sharp kitchen scissors.
4. Grease the inside of the tin and place one circle of paper in the base. Grease the paper if greaseproof.
5. Place the 2 long strips in the tin, pressing them against the sides with the cut flaps against the base; grease the side paper. Place the second circle of paper onto the base of the tin and grease well.

To line a shallow oblong tin
1. Cut a piece of non-stick or grease-proof paper 7.5 cm (3 inches) larger than the size of the tin.
2. Place the tin on the paper and draw round the base on the tin. Make cuts at each corner of the paper to the marked line.
3. Grease the tin and put the paper in, pressing it neatly into the corners and overlapping the cuts in the paper. Grease the paper if greaseproof.

Cake boards
Round and square cake boards ranging from 17.5 cm (7 inches)-40 cm (16 inches) are readily available from department stores. Other shapes available from specialist suppliers and some department stores include the heart and the hexagon. Cake boards are usually finished in silver, but gold boards are also available. These cake boards are ideal for special occasions, but a wooden bread or meat board covered with ordinary kitchen foil is quite adequate for a child's party cake or an informal tea-party.

BASIC CAKE RECIPES

Whisked sponge

2 eggs
50 g (2 oz) caster sugar
50 g (2 oz) plain flour
½ tsp baking powder

Heat the oven to 180°C, 350°F, Gas Mark 4. Grease and base-line with greased greaseproof paper, two 18 cm (7 inch) sandwich tins.

Place the eggs and sugar in a bowl set over a saucepan of hot water and whisk until the mixture is light and thick and leaves a trail when the whisk is lifted (the hot water is not necessary when using an electric whisk.) Remove from the heat and whisk for a further 2 minutes.

Sift the flour with the baking powder into the bowl. Fold carefully into the mixture, using a large metal spoon.

Divide the mixture between the two prepared tins. Shake the tins to level the surface. Bake in the oven for 20-25 minutes until lightly browned and firm to the touch.

Loosen the edges of the cake with the fingertips or a spatula, then turn out on to a wire rack, remove the lining paper and leave to cool completely. Sandwich the cakes together with jam and/or cream, sliced fruit or butter icing.

Variations
Lemon or Orange Whisked Sponge: add the grated rind of ½ lemon or orange with the flour.
Chocolate Whisked Sponge: replace 15 g (½ oz) of the flour with sifted cocoa.
Coffee Whisked Sponge: add 2 tsp instant coffee powder with the flour.

Swiss roll

3 eggs
75 g (3 oz) caster sugar
75 g (3 oz) plain flour
½ tsp baking powder
caster sugar, for sprinkling
6 tbls strawberry jam, warmed

Heat the oven to 200°C, 400°F, Gas Mark 6. Grease and line with greased greaseproof paper a 33 cm × 23 cm (13 inch × 9 inch) shallow tin.

Place the eggs and sugar in a bowl set over a saucepan of hot water and whisk until the mixture is light and thick and leaves a trail when the whisk is lifted (the hot water is not necessary when using an electric whisk). Remove from the heat and whisk for a further 2 minutes.

Sift the flour with the baking powder into a mixing bowl and carefully fold

into the egg mixture, using a large metal spoon.

Pour the mixture into the prepared tin. Shake the tin to level the surface. Bake in the oven for 10-12 minutes until lightly browned and firm to the touch.

Spread a large piece of greaseproof paper on a work surface and sprinkle evenly with caster sugar. Turn the cake out on to the paper and remove the lining paper. Trim the edges neatly and quickly spread the cake with the jam. Roll up from one short end, using the sugared paper to help you. Leave to cool, then carefully unroll, remove the paper, spread with whipped cream and roll up again. For cream fillings, roll the cake with a sheet of greaseproof paper inside. Cool, then add filling.

Basic quick mix cake

This mixture can be baked in many shapes and sizes of tins and is the base for many of the novelty cakes.

100 g (4 oz) quantity
100 g (4 oz) caster sugar
100 g (4 oz) soft margarine
2 eggs
100 g (4 oz) self-raising flour
1 tsp baking powder
175 g (6 oz) quantity
175 g (6 oz) caster sugar
175 g (6 oz) soft margarine
3 eggs
175 g (6 oz) self-raising flour
1½ tsp baking powder

Heat the oven to 160°C, 325°F, Gas Mark 3. Grease and base-line tins.

Place all the cake ingredients in a mixing bowl. Beat with a wooden spoon for 2-3 minutes, then beat well until the mixture is light and fluffy. (Or beat with an electric hand mixer for 1 minute.)

Turn mixture into prepared tin(s) and smooth top(s). Bake for specified cooking time (see below) until cake is golden brown and firm to touch.

Turn the cake on to a wire rack, remove the lining paper, leave to cool completely.

Tins and times for 100 g (4 oz) mixture
2 × 18 cm (7 inch) sandwich tins 25-30 minutes
18 paper cake cases 12-15 minutes
20 cm (8 inch) sandwich tin 35-40 minutes
20 cm (8 inch) ring mould 35-40 minutes
18 cm (7 inch) deep square cake tin 35-40 minutes
900 ml (1½ pint) pudding basin 50 minutes
Tin sizes and cooking times for 175 g (6 oz) mixture
26 paper cake cases 12-15 minutes
2 × 20 cm (8 inch) sandwich tins 30-35 minutes
1 × 23 cm (9 inch) sandwich tin 35 minutes
28 cm × 18 cm (11 inch × 7 inch) shallow oblong tin 35-40 minutes
20 cm (8 inch) round cake tin 35-40 minutes
20 cm (8 inch) square cake tin 35-40 minutes
1.2 litre (2 pint) pudding basin 1 hour

Flavour variations
Chocolate: 100 g (4 oz) mixture, blend 1 tbls cocoa with 1 tbls boiling water and add to cake ingredients.
175 g (6 oz) mixture, blend 2 tbls cocoa with 2 tbls boiling water and add to cake ingredients.
Orange/Lemon: 100 g (4 oz) mixture, add 2 tsp finely grated orange or lemon rind to cake ingredients.
175 g (6 oz) mixture, add 1 tbls finely grated orange or lemon rind.

RICH FRUIT CAKE INGREDIENTS

Round	15cm/6inch	18cm/7inch	20cm/8inch	23cm/9inch	25cm/10inch
Square	13cm/5inch	15cm/6inch	18cm/7inch	20cm/8inch	23cm/9inch
currants	150g/5oz	225g/8oz	350g/12oz	450g/1lb	625g/1lb 6oz
sultanas	50g/2oz	90g/3½oz	120g/4½oz	200g/7oz	225g/8oz
raisins	50g/2oz	90g/3½oz	120g/4½oz	200g/7oz	225g/8oz
glacé cherries	40g/1½oz	65g/2½oz	75g/3oz	100g/4oz	150g/5oz
cut mixed peel	25g/1oz	50g/2oz	50g/2oz	75g/3oz	100g/4oz
blanched almonds	25g/1oz	50g/2oz	50g/2oz	75g/3oz	100g/4oz
lemons	¼	½	¾	1	1
plain flour	90g/3½oz	175g/6oz	200g/7½oz	350g/12oz	400g/14oz
ground cinnamon	½tsp	½tsp	¾tsp	1tsp	1½tsp
ground nutmeg	¼tsp	¼tsp	½tsp	½tsp	¾tsp
ground mixed spice	¼tsp	¼tsp	½tsp	½tsp	¾tsp
butter	75g/3oz	150g/5oz	175g/6oz	275g/10oz	350g/12oz
soft dark brown sugar	75g/3oz	150g/5oz	175g/6oz	275g/10oz	350g/12oz
size 2 eggs	1½	2½	3	5	6
Cooking time (approx)	2 hours	2½ hours	2¾ hours	3¼ hours	3¾ hours
Brandy or sherry (optional)	2 tbls	3 tbls	3 tbls	4 tbls	5 tbls

This rich fruit cake recipe is suitable for Christmas, wedding and other formal special occasion cakes. Rich fruit cakes improve with keeping, which allows the flavours to mature, so bake the cake at least 2 months before it is required.

For a delicious whisky-flavoured fruit cake, substitute Scotch whisky for the brandy or sherry.

It is very important to rinse and thoroughly dry the glacé cherries before adding to the dried fruit, to prevent them sinking during baking.

Rich fruit cake

Heat the oven to 150°C, 300°F, Gas Mark 2. Grease and double line the tin(s) (see pages 6-7 for instructions).

Combine the currants, sultanas and raisins. Cut the glacé cherries into quarters, rinse under warm water and dry carefully with kitchen paper. Add to the dried fruit with the mixed peel. Chop the almonds and finely grate the lemon rind and add to the mixture, stirring well. Sift together the flour and spices.

Beat the butter until softened, then add the sugar and beat well for about 5 minutes until light and fluffy. Beat the eggs lightly and add to the creamed mixture a little at a time, beating well after each addition. Add a little of the sifted flour with each addition of egg to prevent it curdling.

Fold in the remaining flour, followed by the dried fruit mixture. Turn the mixture into the prepared tin(s) and smooth the top. Tie a double thickness of brown paper around the tin.

Bake for the specified cooking time (see chart), checking the cake 30 minutes before the end of the cooking time. To test, insert a fine skewer into the centre of the cake; if it comes out clean the cake is cooked.

Remove the cake from the oven and allow to cool in the tin. Then turn out, remove the lining paper and cool completely on a wire rack. Prick the top of the cake all over with a skewer and spoon the brandy or sherry, if using, evenly over the top. Wrap the cake in greaseproof paper, then over-wrap in foil and store in a cool dry place for up to 3 months. Add more brandy at monthly intervals if liked.

28cm/11inch	30cm/12inch	
25cm/10inch	28cm/11inch	30cm/12inch
300g/1lb 12oz	1.2kg/2lb 8oz	1.5kg/3lb
375g/13oz	400g/14oz	500g/1lb 2oz
375g/13oz	400g/14oz	500g/1lb 2oz
225g/8oz	300g/11oz	350g/12oz
150g/5oz	200g/7oz	250g/9oz
150g/5oz	200g/7oz	250g/9oz
1	1½	2
600g/1lb 5oz	700g/1lb 8oz	825g/1lb 13oz
2tsp	2½tsp	2¾tsp
1tsp	1¼tsp	1½tsp
1tsp	1¼tsp	1½tsp
500g/1lb 2oz	600g/1lb 5oz	800g/1lb 12oz
500g/1lb 2oz	600g/1lb 5oz	800g/1lb 12oz
9	11	14
4¼ hours	5¼ hours	6 hours
6tbls	7tbls	8tbls

• Ranged right and below: a variety of dried and crystallized fruits, nuts, spices and fresh zest. All will be useful in making or decorating cakes

BASIC ICING RECIPES

Butter icing

100 g (4 oz) unsalted butter, softened
225 g (8 oz) icing sugar, sifted
2 tsp lemon juice or milk

Place the butter, icing sugar and lemon juice in a bowl and beat to mix. Beat well with a wooden spoon for about 2 minutes, until light and fluffy.

Variations
Chocolate: Blend 1 tbls cocoa with 1 tbls boiling water to a smooth paste. Beat together with the icing.
Coffee: Replace lemon juice with coffee essence or add 1 tsp instant coffee powder, blended with 1 tsp hot water.
Lemon or Orange: Use strained lemon or orange juice to mix and add 1 tsp finely grated lemon or orange rind and a few drops of food colouring if liked.
Vanilla: Add ½ tsp vanilla essence.

Glacé icing

This simple icing can be used to coat cakes, small cakes and biscuits. It can be made thicker for piping. This quantity will coat the top of a 20 cm (8 inch) cake or ice 18 small cakes.

225 g (8 oz) icing sugar
2-3 tbls boiling water
food colouring (optional)

Sift the icing sugar into a bowl. Gradually beat in enough water to give a smooth shiny icing which will coat the back of the spoon. Add extra water or icing sugar if necessary. Add a few drops food colouring if liked. Use icing immediately.

Variations
Lemon or Orange: Use strained orange or lemon juice instead of water.
Coffee: Replace the water with strong black coffee.
Chocolate: Mix 2 tsp cocoa with the water before adding to the icing sugar.

Moulding icing

This icing is simple to make and can be coloured and used to make moulded decorations, animals, flowers, etc. This quantity will cover the top and sides of a 20 cm (8 inch) round cake.

450 g (1 lb) icing sugar
1 egg white, lightly beaten
1 tbls liquid glucose or glucose syrup

Sift the icing sugar into a bowl. Add the egg white and the glucose and mix together with a wooden spoon until it forms a soft 'dough'. Knead well with the fingers until smooth.

Turn on to a surface sprinkled with icing sugar and continue kneading until the icing is pliable and silky.

Store the icing in a well sealed polythene bag to prevent it drying out.

American frosting

American frosting is a good alternative to royal icing for Christmas cakes or could be used instead of moulding icing for the Valentine sweetheart cake on page 44. This quantity will fill and frost the top and sides of a 20 cm (8 inch) round cake.

175 g (6 oz) caster sugar
1 egg white
2 tbls hot water
pinch of cream of tartar
food colouring (optional)

Place all the ingredients, except the food colouring, in a bowl set over a saucepan of hot water. Whisk until the mixture thickens and soft peaks form when the whisk is lifted.

Remove the bowl from the saucepan and whisk in a few drops of food colouring if liked.

Spread the icing quickly over the cake, forming swirls or peaks with a round ended knife or palette knife.

Royal icing

When making royal icing for a wedding cake it is best to make it up in no more than 900 g (2 lb) batches. It can be stored in a sealed plastic container until ready to use. For coating a cake the icing should form soft peaks, and for piping it should form stiff peaks.

Glycerine is added to soften the icing and make cutting easier, but for a tiered wedding cake it is best to omit it as the icing will need to take the weight of the other tiers.

2 egg whites
450 g (1 lb) icing sugar, sifted
1 tsp lemon juice
1 tsp glycerine (optional)

Beat the egg whites lightly, then gradually beat in half the icing sugar, using a wooden spoon.

Add the lemon juice, the glycerine, if using, and half the remaining sugar. Beat well until smooth and very white.

Gradually beat in sufficient of the remaining icing sugar to give a consistency which will stand in soft peaks.

Place the icing in an airtight container or cover the bowl with a damp cloth and leave for several hours, if possible, to allow the air bubbles to come to the surface and disperse.

Marzipan

Marzipan is easy to make and has a better flavour than the bought variety. If you do use commercially prepared marzipan for a wedding cake, use the white variety, as yellow marzipan can stain the royal icing and spoil the appearance of the cake if some is to be kept after the wedding.

These quantities make 900 g (2 lb) marzipan, sufficient to cover the top and sides of a 20 cm (8 inch) round or square cake.

450 g (1 lb) ground almonds
225 g (8 oz) icing sugar, sifted
225 g (8 oz) caster sugar
2 eggs or 4 egg yolks
½ tsp almond essence
1 tsp lemon juice

Mix the almonds with the sugars. Beat the eggs or yolks with the almond essence and lemon juice. Stir into the almond mixture and mix to a firm paste. Cover to prevent drying.

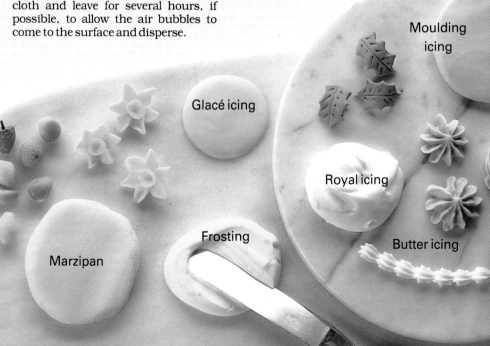

Moulding icing

Glacé icing

Royal icing

Butter icing

Frosting

Marzipan

HOW TO COVER A CAKE WITH MARZIPAN

This method applies to both round and square cakes.

1 Brush the top of the cake with warmed, sieved apricot jam.

2 Invert the cake on to the rolled-out marzipan, which should be 2.5 cm (1 inch) larger than the top of the cake. Using a small palette knife or round-ended knife, press the marzipan against the sides of the cake, to give an even edge to the top of the cake.

3 Turn the cake, right side up, on a cake board. Cut two pieces of string, one the height of the cake and the other the circumference. Brush the sides of the cake with apricot jam.

4 Roll out the remaining marzipan to a rectangle to fit around the cake, using the string as a guide. Using a sharp knife, trim off the excess marzipan. Alternatively, cut the rectangle in half if you find the shorter pieces easier to handle.

5 Loosely roll up the marzipan strip. Then unroll it carefully on to the sides of the cake, pressing it evenly on to the cake.

6 Using a small palette knife, smooth the joins in the marzipan on the sides and top edge of the cake. Reserve the trimmings from the rolled-out marzipan and use these to make cake decorations. Store the cake uncovered in a warm, dry place for at least 48 hours. A tiered wedding cake will require a week to dry.

Marzipan cake decorations may be moulded or cut out. Moulded decorations may include all kinds of animals – elephants, cats, rabbits, mice or Easter chicks – tinted with appropriate food colouring. Make a marzipan snowman, complete with hat and muffler (see page 49) for a Christmas cake, and small marzipan eggs for an Easter cake. Marzipan makes successful moulded flower decorations – roses, daffodils (see page 19), primroses, daisies – as well as fruits for a Christmas cake (see page 18). Cut-out marzipan decorations may include Christmas trees, mistletoe, stars and horseshoes as well as holly leaves, to which berries moulded from red-tinted marzipan may be added. Tie red ribbon around the cake to finish.

HOW TO COVER A CAKE WITH ROYAL ICING

Royal icing, most generally used to ice rich fruit cakes, is always applied over a covering of marzipan.

To achieve the best results cover the cake with two or three thin layers of icing rather than one thick one. This way you will find it easier to make the icing smooth. Ensure that each layer is dry before applying another one. When icing wedding cakes three coats are needed with an extra coat on the top for the lower tiers. For a single tier cake two coats are usually sufficient. Only royal icing is suitable for wedding cakes: no other icing is firm enough to support the weight of the tiers.

To ice the top of the cake

It is essential that the cake does not move during icing. To ensure this, attach the cake to a cake board with a little icing. Put a quantity of icing on top in the centre of the cake and smooth it out with a palette knife, using a paddling movement to spread the icing evenly. Remove surplus icing from the edges with each coating.

Steadily draw an icing ruler or long palette knife across the cake towards you, keeping it at a 30° angle to the top of the cake.

Remove surplus icing from the sides of the cake with the palette knife. If the icing is not sufficiently smooth, spread a little more icing over the cake and draw the ruler over the cake again. Leave to dry completely before applying the next coat. This can take anything up to 24 hours: always allow plenty of time for a really professional finish.

To ice the sides of a round cake

Place the cake on an icing turntable or an upturned plate or bowl. Spread a thin but even layer of icing all round the sides of the cake. Use a paddling action with the palette knife, icing comb or scraper to press out as much air as possible from the icing and prevent unsightly bubbles from forming.

Hold an icing comb or scraper at a 45° angle to the cake. Start at the back of the cake, with your free hand slowly rotate the cake, at the same time move the comb slowly and evenly round the sides of the cake. Remove the comb sharply so the join is hardly noticeable.

Remove any excess icing from the top of the cake with a palette knife, again rotating the cake. If the icing is not smooth enough, wipe the comb and start again. Once the cake is fully iced, allow to dry completely (allow 24 hours for this) before adding the decorations.

To ice the sides of a square-shaped cake

For a square cake, the best way to achieve good corners is to ice opposite sides first. Leave to dry, then ice the remaining two sides.

Spread some icing on one side, then draw the comb or scraper towards you, keeping the cake still to achieve even results. Cut off the icing down the corners, and also on the top and base of the cake. Repeat with the opposite side and leave to dry.

Repeat the process to cover the other two sides, keeping the corners neat and tidy, and leave to dry.

15

HOW TO COVER A CAKE WITH MOULDING ICING

Attach moulding icing to a marzipan-covered cake such as a rich fruit cake, or use it to cover a lighter cake, first brushing the cake with warmed sieved apricot jam to make it stick.
1 Knead the icing until it is smooth and silky. Roll out on a surface sprinkled with icing sugar to a round or square 5 cm (2 inches) larger than cake.
2 Support the icing on a rolling pin and place it carefully over the cake. Press the icing on to the sides of the cake to cover evenly.
3 Dip your hands in cornflour and rub them over the cake until it is smooth and even. Trim off excess icing with a small sharp knife.

For square-shaped cakes
Cut a segment of icing at each corner and mould carefully until corners are even. Leave to dry.

SIX BASIC PIPING NOZZLES

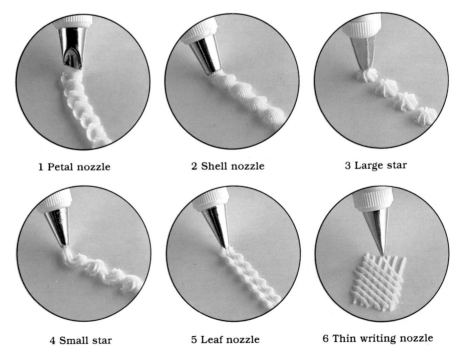

1 Petal nozzle

2 Shell nozzle

3 Large star

4 Small star

5 Leaf nozzle

6 Thin writing nozzle

16

HOW TO MAKE AND USE A PIPING BAG

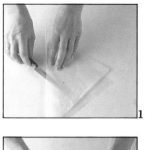

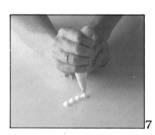

1 To make two icing bags, fold a 25 × 19 cm (10 × 7½ inch) sheet of grease-proof paper in half diagonally, to make two triangles. Cut along fold line, so both triangles have peaks off centre, leaving unequal lengths of paper either side.

2 Position paper triangle so that peak points towards you and long straight edge away. Take outer, right-hand point which is shorter than left hand point and fold inwards, to meet the triangle point facing you, making a cone shape.

3 Pinch cone in place between finger and thumb and draw remaining longer, left-hand flap of paper round cone so that outer point meets point facing you at back.

4 Pinch 3 points together and fold inwards about 3.5 cm (1½ inches) down into cone, to hold cone together.

5 Snip the point of the cone off with scissors, insert your chosen nozzle and three-quarters fill the bag with icing.

6 Fold both outer corners of the top of the icing bag inwards and fold over again to prevent icing escaping.

7 For single applications of icing, like stars, clutch bag in one fist and support and guide with other hand as shown, holding bag and nozzle vertically.

8 For finer icing, such as trellis work and writing with a thin nozzle, pinch bag between index and second finger and gradually push icing down and out with thumb. Hold bag at low writing angle and use other hand to add pressure and steady writing hand.

9 For larger quantities of icing using larger nozzles, a bought nylon icing bag can be used. Three-quarters fill, give a single twist and hold as shown. These bags are washable and can be reused.

CAKE DECORATIONS

Ready-made decorations

Edible decorations such as sweets, dragees (shiny hard sugar balls), mimosa balls, jelly shapes and sugar strands can be used to decorate sponge cakes, children's birthday cakes and novelty cakes. Press chocolate vermicelli or multi-coloured hundreds and thousands on to the side of the cake for a quick finish, or use chopped nuts or toasted coconut. Desiccated coconut can be tinted with food colouring to produce decorative effects. Simply add a few drops of food colouring to the coconut in a bowl and mix together until evenly coloured.

Chocolate coins, a variety of candy bars, chocolate buttons and other favourite sweets can all be used for decoration. For birthdays, plan your cake around a hobby or a special interest the child may have, and here a toy shop may help. Football figures, farm animals, space men and other small shapes can be used to make the cake extra special. Card shops and stationers as

well as specialist shops sell an increasing range of decorations for special occasions such as Christmas, Easter, weddings and engagements.

Making your own simple decorations

Making your own decorations from marzipan or moulding icing can be great fun and very rewarding. To colour the icing place a little on a saucer and knead in the food colouring a few drops at a time.

Marzipan or moulding icing fruits are simple to make. Shape orange icing into a ball and roll in granulated sugar to make an orange. Press a clove into the top to make a stalk. Use green or red icing to make apples in the same way. Make small strawberry shapes from red icing. Shape a small piece of green icing for the hull and press a clove through the top. Make tiny green balls and cluster them to make a bunch of grapes around a 'stem' shape. Shape bananas from yellow icing and press a clove in to one end. Use cocoa blended to a smooth

paste with hot water to brush lines down the banana for markings. Use blue and red colouring to make purple plums, making the ridge with the back of a knife.

Simple flowers can be made by cutting out circles of coloured marzipan or moulding icing. Mould them around a small ball of uncoloured marzipan to form petals. Snip the edge of each petal or curl them outwards. To make daffodils, use marzipan or coloured moulding icing. Curl a small strip of icing around to form the trumpet of the flower. Make five or six pointed petals and stick them around the trumpet, curling them outwards. When they are dry, paint around the top of the trumpet with orange food colouring.

Other simple flowers can be made from one circle of icing, Snip around the edge of circle and overlap each snipped piece. Make contrasting coloured icing beads and place in centre.

Strawberry feather bar cake

For the cake
100g (4oz) caster sugar
100g (4oz) soft margarine
2 eggs
100g (4oz) self-raising flour
1 tsp baking powder
For the filling
75g (3oz) unsalted butter, softened
175g (6oz) icing sugar, sifted
1 tbls milk
red food colouring
2 tbls strawberry jam
For the decoration
100g (4oz) icing sugar, sifted
1-2 tbls boiling water
strawberry flavour dessert sauce

Heat the oven to 160°C, 325°F, Gas Mark 3. Grease and line with greased greaseproof paper a 20cm (8 inch) square cake tin.

Place all the cake ingredients in a mixing bowl and beat with a wooden spoon for about 2 minutes until light and fluffy. Spoon the mixture into the prepared tin and smooth the top.

Bake the cake in the oven for 30-35 minutes until golden brown and firm to the touch. Turn out on to a wire rack, remove the lining paper and leave to cool completely.

To make the filling, place the butter, icing sugar and milk in a bowl. Mix together with a wooden spoon then beat for about 3 minutes until light and fluffy. Tint the buttercream pink with a few drops of food colouring.

Cut the cake in half, then split each half horizontally. Sandwich the split cakes together with strawberry jam, then sandwich the two cakes together with a little butter icing to form a 20cm (8 inch) bar.

To decorate the cake, beat the icing sugar with the water in a bowl until it thickly coats the back of a spoon. Spread the icing over the top of the cake. Place a little dessert sauce in a greaseproof paper piping bag fitted with a thin writing nozzle. Pipe lines of sauce across the icing. Draw a fine skewer across the lines of sauce in alternate directions to form a feather pattern.

Allow the icing to set, then place the remaining butter cream in a piping bag fitted with a shell or star nozzle. Pipe shells around the top edge of the cake and leave to set.

Lacy sugar cake

For the cake
175g (6oz) caster sugar
175g (6oz) soft margarine
3 eggs
175g (6oz) self-raising flour
1½ tsp baking powder
finely grated rind of 1 orange
For the filling and decoration
6 tbls apricot jam, warmed and sieved
75g (3oz) chopped nuts, toasted
icing sugar, sifted

Heat the oven to 160°C, 325°F, Gas Mark 3. Grease and base-line with greased greaseproof paper two 20cm (8 inch) sandwich tins.

Place all the cake ingredients in a mixing bowl and beat with a wooden spoon for about 2 minutes until light and fluffy. Divide the mixture equally between the prepared tins and smooth the tops.

Bake the cakes in the oven for 30-35 minutes until golden brown and firm to the touch. Turn out onto a wire rack, remove the lining paper and leave to cool completely.

● Top: Lacy sugar cake; Bottom: Strawberry feather bar cake

Sandwich the cakes together with two-thirds of the jam. Spread the remaining jam over the side of the cake. Spread the nuts over a sheet of greaseproof paper. Holding the cake carefully on its side, roll in the nuts until well coated.

Place the cake on a serving plate.

Place a patterned doily on top of the cake. Dredge the cake with icing sugar, then very carefully lift off the doily to reveal the sugar pattern.

Variation: Instead of using chopped nuts, coat the side of cake with the same weight of grated chocolate.

Iced fancies

If you have time, make the cake the day before it is to be iced to make cutting it easier.

For the cake
3 eggs
75 g (3 oz) caster sugar
75 g (3 oz) plain flour
½ tsp baking powder
For the icing and decoration
225 g (8 oz) apricot jam, warmed and sieved
225 g (8 oz) marzipan
750 g (1½ lb) icing sugar, sifted
boiling water
red, yellow, orange, green and blue food colouring
angelica, jelly sweets, dragees and mimosa balls

Heat the oven to 180°C, 350°F, Gas Mark 4. Grease and line with greased greaseproof paper a 28 × 18 cm (11 × 7 inch) shallow tin.

Place the eggs and caster sugar in a bowl set over a saucepan of hot water. Whisk until the mixture is thick and pale and leaves a trail when the whisk is lifted. Remove the bowl from the pan and whisk for a further 2 minutes.

Sift the flour with the baking powder and carefully fold it in to the egg mixture, using a metal spoon, until evenly mixed. Pour into the prepared tin.

Bake the cake in the oven for 25-30 minutes until golden brown and firm to the touch. Turn out on to a wire rack, remove the lining paper and leave to cool completely.

Brush the top of the cake with some of the jam. Roll out the marzipan and use to cover the top of the cake. Trim the edges of the cake neatly with a sharp knife, reserving the marzipan trimmings for decoration.

Cut the cake into rounds, triangles, bars and squares. See the diagram opposite for the most economical way to cut the cake.

Brush all the small cakes with the jam. Knead the marzipan trimmings and shape into small rolls and balls.

Place on a few of the cakes to give a raised surface when iced. (Sponge trimmings, cut to shape, can be used for the same effect.)

Place 450 g (1 lb) of the icing sugar in a bowl set over a saucepan of hot water. Beat in enough boiling water until the icing thickly coats the back of a wooden spoon and is of a smooth pouring consistency.

Divide the icing into 6 portions. Keep 1 white and colour the others pink, yellow, orange, blue and green. Place 1 cake of each shape on a wire rack over a tray. Using a tablespoon, coat the cakes with white icing then transfer them to a board. Ice the remaining cakes in this way in the different colours, but remember there are only 4 square cakes.

Mix the remaining icing sugar with boiling water to make icing of a piping consistency. Tint half pink. Fill a piping bag fitted with a thin writing nozzle with white icing and pipe threads of icing across half the cakes. Pipe pink icing threads on the remaining cakes. Decorate the cakes with angelica leaves, jelly sweets, dragees and mimosa balls.

Tortoises

MAKES 18

For the cake
1 tbls cocoa
1 tbls boiling water
100 g (4 oz) caster sugar
100 g (4 oz) soft margarine
2 eggs
100 g (4 oz) self-raising flour
1 tsp baking powder
18 paper cake cases
For the icing and decoration
350 g (12 oz) marzipan
green food colouring
2 tbls apricot jam, warmed and sieved
75 g (3 oz) chocolate
silver dragees

Heat the oven to 190°C, 375°F, Gas Mark 5. Blend the cocoa and water to a smooth paste. Allow to cool. Place in a

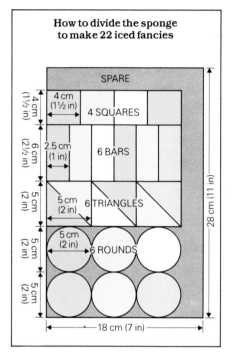

**How to divide the sponge
to make 22 iced fancies**

SPARE

4 cm
(1½ in)   4 SQUARES

2.5 cm
(1 in)   6 BARS

5 cm
(2 in)   6 TRIANGLES

5 cm
(2 in)   6 ROUNDS

4 cm (1½ in)
6 cm (2½ in)
5 cm (2 in)
5 cm (2 in)
5 cm (2 in)

28 cm (11 in)

18 cm (7 in)

bowl with the remaining cake ingredients. Beat with a wooden spoon for about 2 minutes, until light and fluffy.

Divide the mixture between 18 paper cake cases placed in bun tins. Bake in

the oven for 12-15 minutes, until firm to the touch, then allow to cool.

Knead the marzipan on a board until pliable, then gradually knead in food colouring to tint it green.

Roll out two-thirds of the marzipan and cut into 9 cm (3½ inch) rounds, reserving the trimmings. Remove the cakes from the paper cases and invert on to a board. Brush each cake with jam and cover with a marzipan round.

Shape the remaining marzipan into small rolls, flatten slightly and attach to the body to form the head and feet. Score the feet with a small sharp knife. Press silver dragees into the head for the eyes. Score the body into hexagonal tortoise-shell markings.

Melt the chocolate in a bowl set over a pan of hot water. Place the chocolate in a piping bag fitted with a thin writing nozzle and pipe over the tortoise markings. Leave to set.

Variation: To make hedgehogs, colour the marzipan brown with food colouring. Use all the marzipan to cover the cakes. With sharp pointed scissors, make snips over backs of hedgehogs to form spines. Pinch out the marzipan to make a snout and press in silver dragees for eyes.

Celebration ring cake

For the cake
100g (4 oz) butter, softened
100g (4 oz) caster sugar
2 eggs, beaten
50g (2 oz) ground almonds
a few drops of almond essence
25g (1 oz) almonds, chopped
25g (1 oz) glacé pineapple, sliced
25g (1 oz) crystallized ginger, sliced
50g (2 oz) glacé cherries, quartered
100g (4 oz) plain flour
1 tsp baking powder
For the icing
2 egg whites
1 tsp glycerine
450g (1 lb) icing sugar, sifted
For the decoration
crystallized fruits, glacé cherries and
whole blanched almonds

Heat oven to 140°C, 275°F, Gas Mark 1.
Grease and flour 23cm (9 inch) ring
tin.

Place the butter and sugar in a mixing bowl and beat with a wooden spoon for about 2 minutes until pale and fluffy. Add the eggs, a little at a time, beating well. Stir in ground almonds and almond essence.

Add the chopped almonds, pineapple, ginger and cherries, stirring well to mix. Sift flour with baking powder and fold in carefully with metal spoon.

Spoon the mixture into the prepared tin, pressing it down well. Bake the cake in the oven for about 2½ hours until golden brown and firm to the touch. Remove from the oven and allow to cool in the tin for 10 minutes, then turn out on to a wire rack and leave to cool completely.

To make the icing, place the egg whites and glycerine in a bowl and whisk lightly with a fork. Stir in enough icing sugar to make a soft icing, then beat with a wooden spoon or whisk, adding the icing sugar a little at a time until soft peaks form.

Spread the icing evenly over the cake, swirling it with a round-ended knife. Decorate the top with pieces of crystallized fruit and nuts.

Sachertorte

For the cake
175g (6 oz) butter, softened
175g (6 oz) caster sugar
175g (6 oz) plain chocolate, melted
8 eggs, separated
125g (5 oz) plain flour, sifted
For the filling and icing
5 tbls apricot jam, warmed and sieved
225g (8 oz) plain chocolate
2 tbls milk
25g (1 oz) milk chocolate
sugar flowers, to decorate

Heat the oven to 160°C, 325°F, Gas Mark 3. Grease and flour a 23cm (9 inch) round cake tin.

Place the butter and sugar in a mixing bowl and beat with a wooden spoon for about 10 minutes until pale and fluffy. Gradually beat in the chocolate until evenly mixed, then beat in the egg yolks.

Whisk the egg whites stiffly, then fold carefully into the mixture, using a metal spoon. Carefully fold in the sifted flour.

Pour the mixture into the prepared tin. Bake the cake in the oven for 1 hour until firm to the touch. Remove from the oven and allow to cool in the tin for 10 minutes, then turn the cakes out on to a wire rack and leave to cool completely.

Split the cake in half and sandwich together with half the jam. Brush the top and sides with the remaining jam. Melt the plain chocolate in a bowl set over a saucepan of hot water, then remove from the heat and stir in the milk. Pour the chocolate evenly over the cake, using a palette knife to coat the sides. Leave to set.

Melt the milk chocolate in a bowl set over a saucepan of hot water. Place in a greaseproof paper piping bag fitted with a thin writing nozzle. Pipe the word *sacher* in flowing writing over the cake. Decorate with a few sugar flowers, attaching them to the cake with dabs of melted chocolate so that they adhere firmly.

● Top: Sachertorte; Bottom: Celebration ring cake

Coffee walnut gâteau

For the cake
175g (6oz) caster sugar
175g (6oz) soft margarine
3 eggs
175g (6oz) self-raising flour
1½ tsp baking powder
2 tbls strong black coffee
For the butter icing
175g (6oz) unsalted butter, softened
350g (12oz) icing sugar, sifted
3-4 tbls strong black coffee
For the icing and decoration
75g (3oz) walnut halves
100g (4oz) icing sugar, sifted
1-2 tbls strong black coffee

Heat the oven to 160°C, 325°F, Gas Mark 3. Grease and base-line with greased greaseproof paper two 20 cm (8 inch) sandwich tins.

Place all the cake ingredients in a mixing bowl and beat with a wooden spoon for about 2 minutes, until light and fluffy. Divide between the prepared tins and smooth the tops. Bake the cakes in the oven for 30-35 minutes until golden brown and firm to the touch. Turn on to wire rack, remove lining paper and cool completely.

Place all the butter icing ingredients in a mixing bowl and mix together, then beat with a wooden spoon for about 3 minutes, until light and fluffy. Split each cake in half and sandwich the four layers together with two-thirds of the butter icing.

Reserve 8 walnut halves and finely chop the remainder. Spread the sides of the cake with half the remaining butter icing. Spread chopped nuts over a sheet of greaseproof paper. Holding cake carefully on side, roll in nuts to coat. Place the cake on a serving plate.

Place the remaining butter icing in a greaseproof paper piping bag fitted with a small star nozzle. Pipe stars around the edge of the cake. To make the glacé icing, beat the icing sugar with the coffee until smooth and glossy. Pour over top of cake to cover. Decorate with reserved walnut halves and leave to set.

● Left: Black forest gâteau
Right: Coffee walnut gâteau

Black forest gâteau

For the cake
3 eggs
175g (6oz) caster sugar
175g (6oz) plain flour
2 tbls cocoa
2 tsp baking powder
4 tbls hot water
For the filling and decoration
450 ml (¾ pint) whipping cream
3 tbls kirsch
425g (15oz) can cherries, drained or
*   450g (1 lb) fresh cherries, stoned*
100g (4oz) plain chocolate, coarsely
*   grated*
extra whole cherries

Heat the oven to 190°C, 375°F, Gas Mark 5. Grease and line with greased greaseproof paper a 23 cm (9 inch) round cake tin.

Place the eggs and sugar in a bowl set over a saucepan of hot water. Whisk until the mixture is thick and pale and leaves a trail when the whisk is lifted. Remove the bowl from the pan and whisk for a further 2 minutes.

Sift the flour with the cocoa and baking powder on to a plate. Carefully fold into the egg mixture, using a large metal spoon. Gently stir in the hot water. Pour the mixture into the prepared tin. Bake the cake in the oven for 35-40 minutes until well risen and firm to the touch. Carefully turn the cake out on to a wire rack, remove the lining paper and leave to cool completely.

Split the cake into 3 equal layers. Whip the cream stiffly and place one-quarter in a piping bag fitted with a large star nozzle. Sprinkle the bottom layer of cake with a little kirsch and pipe a band of whipped cream around the edge. Spread the stoned cherries evenly around the edge, inside the band of cream.

Place the centre sponge layer on top of the cherries and sprinkle with a little kirsch. Spread with a layer of cream. Sprinkle the underside of the top layer of sponge with the remaining kirsch and invert on to the sponge layer spread with cream.

Spread the top and sides of the cake with the remaining cream and sprinkle with grated chocolate. Pipe whirls of cream around the top of the cake and decorate with whole cherries. Keep the Black forest gâteau in a cool place until ready to serve.

Child's numeral cake

Quick mix cake mixture (see page 9) flavoured as you wish

Jam (optional)
For the icing and decoration
225 g (8 oz) unsalted butter, softened
450 g (1 lb) icing sugar, sifted
1 tbls milk
green food colouring
smarties, other small sweets or
*   decoration of your choice*
candles and candle holders, optional

Children will enjoy these number cakes which can be decorated in many ways, giving plenty of scope for your imagination.
Shaping numeral cakes (see page 9 for quantities of cake mixture and cooking times)
Nought: Bake a 23 cm (9 inch) round cake. When cold, cut a 7.5 cm (3 inch) diameter hole in the centre.
One: Bake a 15 cm (6 inch) square cake. Cut across in 2 halves and place one bar on top of the other. Sandwich together with jam. Or make as diagram.
Two: Bake a 28 × 18 cm (11 × 7 inch) shallow cake. Cut out a pattern in greaseproof paper, transfer to the top of the cake and cut out.
Three: Bake two 20 cm (8 inch) round sandwich cakes. Cut out a pattern in greaseproof paper, transfer to the top of each cake and cut out. Sandwich the 2 cakes together with jam.
Four: Bake a 20 cm (8 inch) square cake. Cut a pattern in greaseproof paper, transfer to the top of the cake and cut out.
Five: Bake a 28 × 18 cm (11 × 7 inch) shallow cake. Cut out a pattern in greaseproof paper, transfer to the top of the cake and cut out.
Six or Nine: Bake a 28 × 18 cm (11 × 7 inch) shallow cake. Cut out a pattern in greaseproof paper, transfer to the top of the cake and cut out.
Seven: Bake a 20 cm (8 inch) square cake. Cut out a pattern in greaseproof paper, transfer to the top of the cake and cut out.
Eight: Bake two 20 cm, (8 inch) round sandwich cakes. Cut a 7.5 cm (3 inch) circle out of the centre of each cake. Trim a piece off the side of each cake and sandwich together with jam, end to end, to make an eight.
If using pairs of cakes, sandwich them together with jam. Place on a cake board. Place the butter, icing sugar and milk in a mixing bowl and beat to mix, then beat well with a wooden spoon for about 2 minutes until light and fluffy. Tint with a few drops of food colouring. Reserving a little butter icing for piping, spread the rest over the top and sides of the cake, swirling decoratively with a round-ended knife. Tint the reserved butter icing a darker shade and place in a greaseproof paper piping bag fitted with a star nozzle. Pipe stars around the top edge and base of the cake.
Decorate the top of the cake with sweets, or pipe a name on top of the cake with a little of the darker butter icing, and position the candles, if using, in a cluster round edge.

● Child's numeral cake: example shown for an eight-year-old

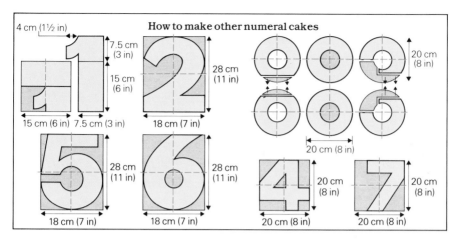

How to make other numeral cakes

4 cm (1½ in)

7.5 cm (3 in)

15 cm (6 in)

15 cm (6 in) 7.5 cm (3 in)

28 cm (11 in)

18 cm (7 in)

20 cm (8 in)

20 cm (8 in)

28 cm (11 in)

18 cm (7 in)

28 cm (11 in)

18 cm (7 in)

20 cm (8 in)

20 cm (8 in)

20 cm (8 in)

20 cm (8 in)

Rocket cake

Double quantity 100g (4 oz) quick mix
cake mixture (see page 9)
For the icing and decoration
4 small bars white chocolate
225 g (8 oz) jam, warmed and sieved
red food colouring
ice cream cone

Heat the oven to 160°C, 325°F, Gas Mark 3. Grease and line with greased greaseproof paper a 20 cm (8 inch) square cake tin. Pour mixture into tin.

Bake the cake mixture in the oven for about 1 hour until golden brown and firm to the touch. Turn out on to a wire rack, remove lining paper. Leave to cool.

Draw a 10 × 10 cm (4 × 4 inches) square on a sheet of kitchen foil or non-stick silicone paper. Melt the white chocolate in a bowl set over a saucepan of hot water and spread within the marked square. Shake gently to level and leave until just set. Using a ruler and sharp knife, trim the edges of the white chocolate, then cut in half, making two squares. Cut each in half to form triangles. Chill until hard.

Following the diagram cut the cake into two 10 cm (4 inch) rounds and two 7.5 cm (3 inch) rounds. Assemble the rocket placing the large rounds on top of each other and trimming the edges to slope the sides. Do the same with the smaller rounds. Then sandwich all the rounds together with jam. Put the assembled cake on a board.

Make the butter icing according to the method on page 12. Tint two-thirds red. Leave the remainder white.

Spread bottom half of cake with red icing and top half with white.

Cut the tip off the ice cream cone. Spread the cone with red icing. Place the iced cone on top of the cake. Place the remaining red icing in a piping bag fitted with a small star nozzle and pipe a few stars over the white section. Pipe more stars round the top and base of the rocket and between the sections. Pipe a door and numeral on the rocket.

Press the chocolate triangles around the base. Place a candle in the top.

How to make the rocket

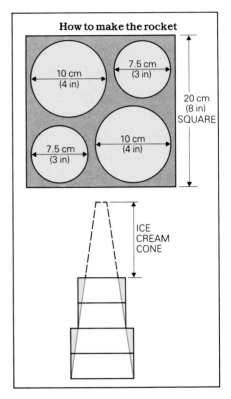

Space Shuttle Cake

1 × 4 egg quantity Swiss roll, using
apricot jam (see page 8)

For the icing and decoration
1½ quantities moulding icing
(see page 12)
cornflour
red and blue food colourings
1 oblong ice cream wafer
1 strip of liquorice
2 liquorice rolls with white centres
1 tbls apricot jam, warmed and sieved

Follow instructions for making the Swiss roll to the point where the edges have been trimmed off the unrolled baked sponge.

Measure from the top right-hand corner 12.5 cm (5 inches) down the long side and 12.5 cm (5 inches) across the top edge. Cut across the corner from these two points and reserve the

• Left: Rocket cake; Right: Space shuttle cake

triangular piece of cake for the 'wings'.

Quickly spread the cake with apricot jam and using the sugared paper to help you, start rolling from the bottom right-hand corner at an angle towards the top left-hand corner, to form a point at one end of the roll. Leave to cool on a wire rack, with the join underneath then carefully remove sugared paper.

Roll out two-thirds moulding icing on a lightly cornfloured surface to an oblong large enough to cover the cake.

Place the cake in the centre of a 30 cm (12 inch) square silver cake board. Mould a small piece of icing into a thick horseshoe shape and place it in position 5 cm (2 inch) in from 'nose end' for the cockpit.

Cover the cake carefully with icing, trim to fit and make neat joins underneath the cake and at the back end, using well-cornfloured fingers.

Shape the cockpit and a pointed 'nose' shape at the sharp end of the cake until smooth.

Cut remaining triangle of cake in half to form the wings. Cut wafer into 2 triangles and trim into tail pieces.

Roll out remaining one-third of icing and cover both sides of the 'wings' and tail pieces, trim to fit and smooth all joins.

Position the wings at the sides of the cake.

Knead the icing trimmings together, and cut in half. Tint one half red and one half blue with food colourings.

Roll out very thin strips of red and blue icing and trim the tail pieces, wings and body of space shuttle. Use a fine paint brush and water to dampen the trimmed edges before fixing on the icing strips.

Cut liquorice into thin strips and trim the cockpit. Thinly slice the liquorice rolls and place in position for the windows. Leave cake to set.

Cut 2 deep slits on top of the cake at the back and fit the tail pieces in position.

See diagram overleaf

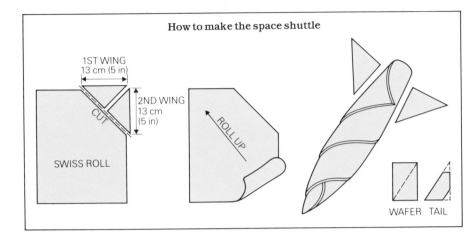

How to make the space shuttle

1ST WING
13 cm (5 in)

2ND WING
13 cm
(5 in)

CUT

SWISS ROLL

ROLL UP

WAFER TAIL

Computer cake

275 g (10 oz) quick mix cake mixture
(see page 9)

For the icing and decoration
4 tbls apricot jam, warmed and sieved
1½ quantities moulding icing (see
    page 12)
brown and blue food colourings
cornflour
1 packet easy to use Decorative Icing
    Alphabet Range in blue
1 packet easy to use Decorative Icing
    Children's Range Train
rainbow coloured dragees

Heat the oven to 160°C, 325°F, Gas
Mark 3. Grease and line a 20 cm (8 inch)
square cake tin and a 28 × 17.5 cm (11
× 7 inch) Swiss roll tin.

Bake two-thirds of the cake mixture
in the prepared square cake tin for 35-
40 minutes. Bake remaining one-third
cake mixture in the prepared Swiss roll
tin for 15-20 minutes. Turn on to wire
rack, remove lining paper and cool.

Place square cake on a 20 cm (8 inch)
thin square silver cake card. Cut a
10 cm (4 inch) × 18 cm (7 inch) rectangle from the oblong cake and reserve
for the keyboard. Cut 4 cm (½ inch) ×
18 cm (7 inch) strips from the remainder of the cake to form frame for screen.

Brush the top of the large square

cake with apricot jam and place the
strips of cake in position to form a
screen, trimming them to fit (see diagram). Trim the sides of the square
cake flush with the screen, if necessary.

Place the reserved piece of oblong
cake on a 10 cm (4 inch) × 18 cm (7
inch) piece of card.

Tint three-quarters of the moulding
icing pale coffee colour with brown food
colouring. Roll out two-thirds of the
icing on a well-cornfloured surface and
place loosely over the square cake.

Cut out and remove a 12.5 cm (5
inch) square of icing from centre and
smooth icing around edge of screen
and down sides of cake. Trim.

Roll out remaining one-third of icing
to cover the small (keyboard) cake,
cover and trim to fit. Knead the trimmings together and colour dark brown.

Roll out and trim icing to a 10 cm (4
inch) square, then cut into 26 × 1 cm
(½ inch) squares and one 5 × 1 cm (2 ×
½ inch) bar. Arrange the squares and
bar on the 'keyboard' cake and secure
the appropriate letters with a little apricot jam. (See photograph.) Trim the top
edges of each cake with thin strips of
brown icing and base with wider strips.

Tint remaining one-quarter of icing
pale blue, roll out and trim to a 16 cm
(6½ inch) square and place in position
for the screen. Decorate the edges of the
screen with dragees. Put train in centre.

● Computer cake

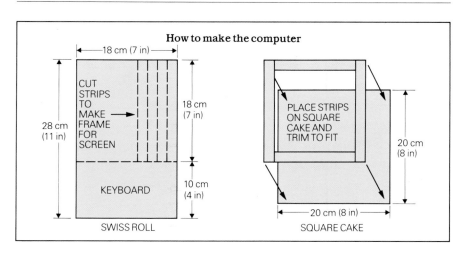

How to make the computer

SWISS ROLL

18 cm (7 in)

28 cm (11 in)

CUT STRIPS TO MAKE FRAME FOR SCREEN

18 cm (7 in)

KEYBOARD

10 cm (4 in)

SQUARE CAKE

PLACE STRIPS ON SQUARE CAKE AND TRIM TO FIT

20 cm (8 in)

20 cm (8 in)

Gingerbread house

For the cake
450 g (1 lb) plain flour
1 tbls ground ginger
1 tbls mixed spice
8 tbls golden syrup
75 g (3 oz) margarine or butter
75 g (3 oz) soft light brown sugar
1 tbls bicarbonate of soda
2 tbls water
1 egg
1 egg yolk
For the icing and decoration
boiled sweets
1 quantity Royal Icing (see page 13)
2 packets small jelly sweets
2 round liquorice allsorts
1 tube smarties
100 g (4 oz) liquorice allsorts
dolly mixtures, coloured dragees,
*   sugar flowers*
miniature torch

Heat the oven to 190°C, 375°F, Gas Mark 5. Line two baking sheets with non-stick silicone paper. Following the diagrams overleaf, cut out thin card shapes for the roof, chimney pieces, base, side and end walls of the house.

Sift the flour with the ginger and spice into a mixing bowl. Place the syrup in a saucepan with the margarine and sugar. Stir over a low heat until melted. Dissolve the bicarbonate of soda in the water in a bowl, then add to the dry ingredients with the syrup mixture, egg and egg yolk. Mix well together with a wooden spoon to form a soft dough.

Roll out the dough to a 5 mm (¼ inch) thickness on a floured board or work surface. Using the card shapes as a guide, cut out 2 end walls, 2 side walls, 2 roof pieces, 2 chimney pieces and a base, reserving the trimmings. Place the cut out shapes on baking sheets. Cut out windows and doors and trim, if necessary, to exact size of cards.

Roll out a small strip of dough and place along the base of one door. Place a boiled sweet in the centre. (This will melt to produce a glass effect.) Place a sweet in each window space.

Bake the dough in the oven for 10 minutes, switching the baking sheets after 5 minutes. Remove from the oven and allow to cool on the baking sheets for 10 minutes, then transfer to a wire rack and leave to cool completely.

Roll out the dough trimmings and cut into 1 × 2.5 cm (½ × 1 inch) pieces for the fence. Bake in the oven as before.

Cover a tray with foil or use a 35 cm (14 inch) square cake board. Place the base piece of the house on the tray and spread the edges with icing. Spread a thin layer of icing on all edges of the side and end walls. Join the side and end walls around the base, press together to secure and hold gently in place for a few minutes until the icing has set a little.

Spread a little icing around the edges of the roof, where it will join the walls, and carefully place the roof in position. Leave to set for at least 1 hour before decorating.

Spread icing over the tray and stick the small baked pieces around the house for the fence. Spread icing on the ridge of the roof and around the edges of the roof to form snow. Sandwich the chimney pieces together with icing. Cut off one corner to fit the roof. Stick in position with icing and spread a little icing around the top of the chimney. Cover the chimney side of house completely with icing.

Fix two liquorice allsorts on to the chimney. Fill a greaseproof paper piping bag with icing and snip off the point. Pipe lines of icing across the un-iced side of the roof. Stick rows of sweets along the icing. Pipe icing around the windows and doors and decorate with sweets. Fix a dragee in place for the door handle. Pipe around the garden and fix dragees on the piping. Place sugar flowers in garden. Pipe 'snow' on top of fence.

Switch on the torch and place it in the house, through the back door. Leave icing to set completely.

● Gingerbread house

34

How to make the gingerbread house

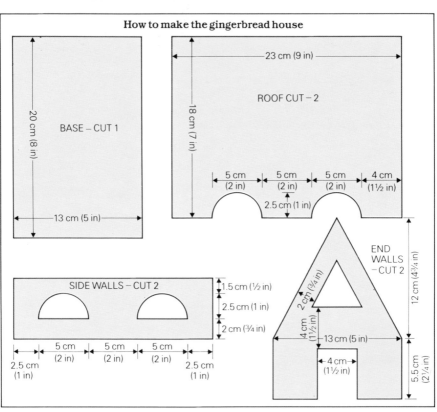

BASE – CUT 1

20 cm (8 in)

13 cm (5 in)

ROOF CUT – 2

23 cm (9 in)

18 cm (7 in)

5 cm (2 in) 5 cm (2 in) 5 cm (2 in) 4 cm (1½ in)

2.5 cm (1 in)

SIDE WALLS – CUT 2

1.5 cm (½ in)

2.5 cm (1 in)

2 cm (¾ in)

2.5 cm (1 in) 5 cm (2 in) 5 cm (2 in) 5 cm (2 in) 2.5 cm (1 in)

END WALLS – CUT 2

12 cm (4¾ in)

2 cm (¾ in)

4 cm (1½ in)

13 cm (5 in)

4 cm (1½ in)

5.5 cm (2¼ in)

● Peppermint racer

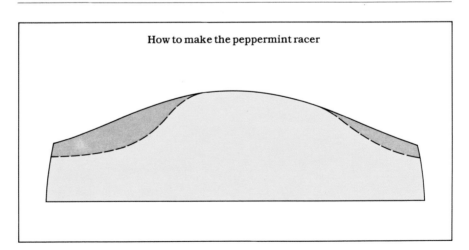

How to make the peppermint racer

Heat the oven to 160°C, 325°F, Gas Mark 3. Grease and line with greased greaseproof paper a 1 kg (2 lb)/1.5 litre (2½ pint) loaf tin.

Pour the cake mixture into the prepared tin and bake in the oven for 50-55 minutes until firm to the touch. Turn out on to a wire rack, remove the lining paper and leave to cool completely.

Make the butter icing, adding peppermint essence to taste, and tint it pale green with food colouring. Cut the cake as shown in the diagram and trim the front corners to shape the body of the car, then brush the cut surfaces with some of the jam. Spread the cake with the butter icing and smooth with a palette knife dipped in hot water.

Spread a cake board or foil-covered board with jam and sprinkle thickly with Demerara sugar. Place the Swiss rolls on the cake board about 10 cm (4 inches) apart to make the axles. Place the cake on top.

Replace the sweets in the centre of each liquorice wheel with a round mint, then press a wheel on to the sides of the car, in front of each axle. Use dragees to outline the front and rear 'wind-screens'. (The easiest way to handle dragees is with a pair of clean tweezers.) Arrange a semi-circle of dragees above each wheel.

Unwind the remaining liquorice wheel and cut four strips to make the front and back bumpers. Cut small strips of liquorice, split in half lengthways and make the windscreen wipers. Make door handles from small bits of liquorice and stick dragees on either side of the handle.

Stick white tooty minties at the front and rear end of the car for the lights. Place a row of green and white tooty minties along one side of the bonnet, roof and boot. Make an exhaust from two pieces of the trimmings, if liked.

To make the number plates, cut 2 small oblongs of rice paper and write the child's name and age on the paper using a food colouring pen. Stick on the front and back ends of the car, and place a white tooty minty to either side. Use the green cocktail stick for the aerial.

Peppermint racer

175 g (6 oz) quantity chocolate quick mix cake mixture (see page 9)

For the icing and decoration
¾ quantity butter icing (see page 12)
peppermint essence
green food colouring
2-3 tbls apricot jam, warmed and
  sieved
Demerara sugar, for sprinkling
2 mini Swiss rolls
5 liquorice catherine wheels
4 round mints
silver or green dragees
white and green tooty minties
rice paper
food colouring pen
1 green plastic cocktail stick

Hickory Dickory Dock cake

Double quantity 100 g (4 oz) quick mix cake mixture (see page 9)

For the icing and decoration

1 quantity moulding icing (see page 12)
red food colouring
3 tbls bramble jelly, warmed and melted
225 g (8 oz) icing sugar, sifted
boiling water
chocolate buttons
2 silver dragees

Heat the oven to 160°C, 325°F, Gas Mark 3. Grease and line with greased greaseproof paper a 20 cm (8 inch) round sandwich tin and an 18 cm (7 inch) square cake tin. Divide the cake mixture between the prepared tins. Bake in the oven for 35-40 minutes, until golden brown and firm to the touch. Turn the cakes out on to a wire rack, remove the lining paper and leave to cool completely.

Knead the moulding icing until pliable, then reserve a small piece to make a mouse and tint the remainder pale pink.

Cut a curved edge from one side of the square cake so that it fits snugly against the round cake. Separate the cakes and brush the top and sides of each with bramble jelly. Reserve a little pink moulding icing and cut the remainder in half. Roll out each half and use to cover the cakes, moulding it round the sides. Place the round cake on a board or foil-covered tray with the square cake fitted below it.

To make the piping icing, put the icing sugar into a bowl with enough boiling water to form a stiff piping consistency. Beat until smooth.

Place the icing in a greaseproof paper piping bag fitted with a star nozzle and pipe stars around the top of the round cake to form the clock face and around the square cake to form the workings. Pipe stars around the base of both cakes.

Attach a chocolate button to the centre of the round cake and place 12 buttons round the edge. Mix the remaining icing sugar with a little water to a piping consistency and place in a greaseproof paper piping bag fitted with a thin writing nozzle. Pipe numbers on the buttons and pipe clock hands to 1 o'clock. Pipe two zig-zag lines of icing on the lower cake to form the pendulum and finish it with 2 chocolate buttons.

Shape the reserved uncoloured piece of moulding icing into a mouse and press in silver dragees for the eyes. Place the mouse on the lower cake.

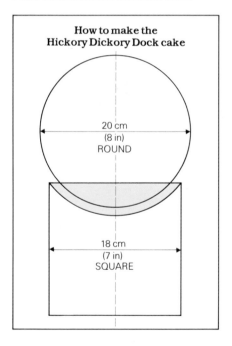

How to make the Hickory Dickory Dock cake

20 cm
(8 in)
ROUND

18 cm
(7 in)
SQUARE

● Hickory Dickory Dock cake

Pirates' treasure chest

175 g (6 oz) orange flavoured quick mix
cake mixture (see page 9)

100 g (4 oz) chocolate dots
25 cm (10 inch) square gold board

For the icing and decoration
50 g (2 oz) chocolate and hazelnut
  spread
gold dragees
1 chocolate covered mini Swiss roll
jelly diamond cake decorations
2 tbls apricot jam, warmed and sieved
coffee sugar crystals, for sprinkling
assorted sweets, including foil-
  covered chocolate coins, sweet
  'jewellery' and gold 'bullion'
pirates' treasure map (optional)
1 rock cake (optional)

Heat the oven to 160°C, 325°F, Gas
Mark 3. Grease and line with greased
greaseproof paper a 1 kg (2 lb)/1.5 litre
(2½ pint) loaf tin.

Make the cake mixture and stir in the
chocolate dots. Pour into the prepared
tin and bake in the oven for about 55
minutes, until golden brown and firm

to the touch. Turn out on to a wire rack,
remove the lining paper and leave right
way up to cool.

Cut a horizontal slice, about 1 cm (½
inch) deep, from the top of the cake to
make the lid of the chest and trim a
narrow strip off one long side. Spread
the sides of the base of the chest with
chocolate and hazelnut spread. Place
on the cake board. Spread the lid with
chocolate and hazelnut spread, leaving
the underside uncovered. Using clean
tweezers, arrange a row of dragees
around the top and bottom edges of the
base and the lid, and down each corner.

Cut a thick slice from the flat side of
the Swiss roll, then place the roll lengthways on top of the base, towards the
front of the centre. Place the lid on the
base, with the trimmed side at the
back. (The Swiss roll will help keep it
open.) Decorate with jelly diamonds.

Spread the area around the base of
the cake with jam and sprinkle with
sugar crystals. Stuff the chest with
chocolate coins and sweet 'jewellery'.
Place a pile of coins, bullion and sweets
around the base of the chest. Use the
rock cake as a pirates' island and stick
with candles, if using.

● Below left: Treasure chest cake; Above: Henry Hedgehog

Henry Hedgehog

175 g (6 oz) quick mix cake mixture, chocolate flavoured (see page 9)

For the icing and decoration
2 tbls cocoa
2 tbls boiling water
100 g (4 oz) unsalted butter, softened
225 g (8 oz) icing sugar, sifted
3 chocolate flake bars
2 brown smarties
1 red smartie

Heat the oven to 160°C, 325°F, Gas Mark 3. Reserve 1 tablespoon of the cake mixture and bake the remainder in a greased 1.2 litre (2 pint) pudding basin in the oven for 1 hour, until risen and firm to the touch. Loosen the sides of the cake with a small round bladed knife and turn out on to a wire rack. Leave to cool completely. Meanwhile, bake reserved cake mixture in paper case for 15 minutes. Leave to cool.

To make the butter icing, blend the cocoa and boiling water to a smooth paste. Allow to cool. Place in a bowl with the butter and icing sugar and beat to mix, then beat well with a wooden spoon for about 2 minutes.

Cut the large cake in half vertically, then turn the 2 halves cut sides down on a board so that the 2 bases meet, to form a hedgehog shape. Split each half in half again horizontally, then sandwich together with one-third of the butter icing.

Cut a small vertical slice from one side of the fairy cake. Place the large piece cut side down on the board, with the top of the fairy cake against one end of the large cake, to form the head. Attach the smaller piece to the other end in the same way, to form the tail.

Spread the remaining butter icing over the cake to cover, shaping one end to a point to form a snout. Roughly crumble the chocolate flake bars and arrange in rows over the cake to form spines, leaving the area around the snout uncovered. Press two brown smarties on to the face for the eyes and a red smartie for the nose. Leave to set.

41

Tooty tug

175 g (6 oz) quantity quick mix cake
mixture (see page 9)
1 large banana, mashed

For the icing and decoration
1 tablet lime jelly, made up
2 tbls apricot jam, warmed and sieved
50 g (2 oz) chocolate, melted
½ quantity vanilla butter icing (see
page 12)
red food colouring
1-2 packets tooty frooties
red food colouring pen and 2 pieces
rice paper (optional)
birthday candles
a few smarties
4 polo mints
2 thin liquorice laces
a little dream topping or whipped
cream (optional)

Heat the oven to 160°C, 325°F, Gas
Mark 3. Grease and line with greased
greaseproof paper an 18 or 20 cm (7 or 8
inch) deep square tin.

Make the cake mixture, adding the
banana. Pour the mixture into the prepared tin and bake in the oven for about
55 minutes until golden brown and
firm to the touch. Remove from the
oven and allow to cool for 5 minutes,
then turn out on to a wire rack, remove
the lining paper and leave to cool
completely.

Trim the cake level if necessary. Cut
out pieces of cake following the diagram. Use a 5 cm (2 inch) plain biscuit
cutter to cut out the round piece. Brush
each piece of cake with jam. Spread
melted chocolate over the top of each
piece and leave to set. (Reserve the remaining chocolate for piping, if liked.)

Tint the icing red and spread around
the sides of each piece of cake. Place the
remaining icing in a piping bag fitted
with a star nozzle.

Place the largest piece of cake on a
shallow dish or tray to make the tug's
hull. Place the middle piece on top, towards the front of the hull, to make the
upper deck. Put the rounded piece on
top of the deck. Pipe a border of butter

icing around the top edge of each piece
of cake.

Stick tooty frooties around the base
of the hull. Place smarties around the
sides of the upper deck for portholes.
Write the child's name and age on each
piece of rice paper and stick on to the
sides of the tug. Alternatively, melt the
remaining chocolate again, place in a
piping bag fitted with a writing tube
and pipe the child's name and age on
either side of the hull. Stick birthday
candles into the top piece, grouping
them close together.

Tie 3 polo mints on each liquorice
lace to make life-savers. Tie the laces
together. Before serving, tie the laces
around the hull. Break up the jelly and
spoon around sides. Decorate with
cream or topping, if using.

How to make the 'tooty tug' cake

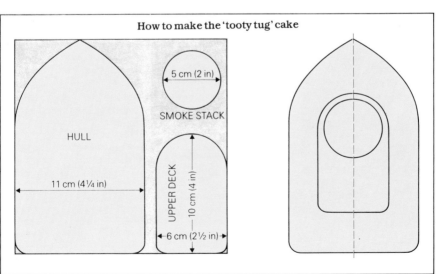

HULL

11 cm (4¼ in)

5 cm (2 in)

SMOKE STACK

UPPER DECK

10 cm (4 in)

6 cm (2½ in)

Valentine sweetheart cake

For a less formal effect, American frosting (see page 12) can be used to ice this cake. Swirl over the top and sides and make circular shapes in the icing with a palette knife.

For the cake
225 g (8 oz) caster sugar
225 g (8 oz) soft margarine
4 eggs
225 g (8 oz) self-raising flour
2 tsp baking powder
finely grated rind of 1 lemon
For the icing and decoration
3 tbls raspberry jam
1½ quantities moulding icing (see page 12)
red food colouring
pink and white rose petals
mint leaves
1 egg white
caster sugar

Heat the oven to 160°C, 325°F, Gas Mark 3. Grease and line with greased greaseproof paper a 23-25 cm (9-10 inch) heart-shaped tin.

Place all the cake ingredients in a mixing bowl and beat to mix, then beat with a wooden spoon for about 2 minutes, until light and fluffy. Turn into the prepared tin and smooth the top. Bake the cake for 45-55 minutes until golden brown and firm to the touch. Turn out on to a wire rack, remove the lining paper and leave to cool completely before icing.

Split the cake in half horizontally and sandwich together with the jam. Tint the moulding icing pink. Use the moulding icing to cover the top and sides and smooth over carefully. Frost the rose petals and mint leaves (see steps) and arrange on top of the cake when dry.

These petals are edible and once dried will keep for 3-4 weeks between layers of tissue paper.

How to crystallize rose petals

1 Check that all the rose petals and leaves are absolutely clean and dry before carefully detaching them from the stem.

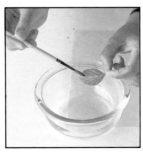

2 Place the egg white in a bowl. Using a fine paint brush, apply lightly to cover petals and leaves, holding them securely between finger and thumb.

3 Spread caster sugar over a sheet of greaseproof paper. Dip in the coated petals and leaves, using a teaspoon to sprinkle evenly with sugar.

• Valentine sweetheart cake

Simnel cake

For the cake
175g (6oz) butter
175g (6oz) caster sugar
3 eggs, beaten
450g (1 lb) mixed dried fruit
50g (2oz) glacé cherries, halved
3 tbls sherry
225g (8oz) plain flour
2 tsp mixed spice
1 tsp baking powder
450g (1 lb) marzipan
1 egg yolk, beaten
For the decoration
marzipan flowers or fruits (see page 13)
yellow ribbon

Heat the oven to 160°C, 325°F, Gas Mark 3. Grease and double line with greased greaseproof paper a 20 cm (8 inch) round cake tin. Place the butter and sugar in a mixing bowl. Beat to mix, then beat well with a wooden spoon for about 5 minutes, until light and fluffy. Beat in the eggs, a little at a time.

Stir in the dried fruit, glacé cherries, and sherry. Sift the flour with the spice and baking powder and fold in lightly, using a large metal spoon.

Roll out half the marzipan to a 20 cm (8 inch) circle. Turn half the cake mixture into the prepared cake tin and smooth the top. Cover with the round of marzipan and top with the remaining cake mixture, smoothing the top. Bake the cake in the oven for 2¼-2½ hours until it is deep golden brown and springs back when pressed with the fingers.

Remove the cake from the oven and allow it to cool in the tin for 15 minutes. Then turn it out on to a wire rack, remove the lining paper and leave it to cool completely. Roll out the remaining marzipan to a circle to fit the top of the cake. Brush the top of the cake with a little egg yolk and place the marzipan on top. Pinch the edges of the marzipan with the fingers and mark the top in a lattice pattern, using a sharp knife. Brush the marzipan with the remain-

ing egg yolk.

Place the cake on a baking sheet under a moderate grill for 5 minutes until the marzipan is lightly browned. Leave to cool, then decorate the top with marzipan fruits or flowers and tie a ribbon around the side.

Easter basket

100g (4oz) quick mix cake mixture, coffee flavoured (see page 9)

For the icing and decoration
2 tbls cocoa
2 tbls boiling water
100g (4oz) unsalted butter, softened
225g (8oz) icing sugar, sifted
75g (3oz) marzipan
aluminium foil
½ metre (18 inch) narrow yellow ribbon

Heat the oven to 160°C, 325°F, Gas Mark 3. Place the mixture in a greased 900 ml (1½ pint) pudding basin and smooth the top, Bake in the oven for 50 minutes until firm to the touch. Turn out on to a wire rack and leave to cool completely.

To make the butter icing, blend the cocoa and boiling water to a smooth paste. Allow it to cool slightly. Place in a bowl with the butter and icing sugar and beat to mix, then beat well with a wooden spoon for about 2 minutes, until light and fluffy.

Split the cake in half horizontally and sandwich together with a little butter icing. Place the cake, smallest end down, on a serving plate or board.

Spread butter icing over the top and sides. Smooth the icing on top of the cake and mark the sides with a fork to resemble a basket weave, or place the remaining icing in a greaseproof paper piping bag fitted with a ribbon nozzle. Pipe a basket weave design and a shell edging around the top of the cake.

Shape the marzipan into daffodils (see page 19) and arrange on top of the basket. To make the handle, fold a strip of foil over several times to form a thick strong band. Wrap the ribbon around the foil and secure at each end with sticky tape. Place the handle on the cake, fixing each end to the icing. Finish the decoration with a bow of yellow satin ribbon.

● Left: Easter basket; Right: Simnel cake

● Snowman Christmas cake

Snowman Christmas cake

For the cake
225g (8oz) seedless raisins
225g (8oz) currants
225g (8oz) sultanas
100g (4oz) cut mixed peel
50g (2oz) blanched almonds,
  chopped
50g (2oz) glacé cherries, washed,
  dried and quartered
grated rind of 1 lemon
225g (8oz) butter, softened
225g (8oz) soft dark brown sugar
4 eggs, beaten
225g (8oz) plain flour
1 tsp mixed spice
½ tsp ground cinnamon
¼ tsp ground nutmeg
2 tbls brandy
For the decoration
4 tbls apricot jam, warmed and sieved
750g (1½lb) marzipan
25 cm (10 inch) silver cake board
royal icing made with 1 kg (2 lb) icing
  sugar (see page 13)
½ quantity moulding icing (see page
  12)
red, green orange and brown food
  colourings
extra icing sugar, sifted

Heat the oven to 150°C, 300°F, Gas Mark 2. Grease and line a 20 cm (8 inch) round deep cake tin (see page 6). Combine the raisins, currants, sultanas, peel, almonds, cherries and lemon rind.

Place the butter and sugar in a mixing bowl, beat to mix, then beat with a wooden spoon for about 5 minutes, until light and fluffy. Beat in the eggs, a little at a time, sifting in a little flour with each addition.

Sift the remaining flour with the spices into the bowl and fold in carefully, using a large metal spoon. Fold in the brandy. Add the fruit mixture and mix well.

Turn the mixture into the prepared tin and smooth the top. Wrap several thicknesses of brown paper or news-paper round the outside of the tin (see p.6) and bake for 3½-3¾ hours until a fine skewer inserted into the centre of the cake comes out clean.

Remove the cake from the oven and allow to cool in the tin, then turn out on to a wire rack and remove the lining paper. Leave to cool completely, then wrap the cake in foil and store in an airtight tin until required.

Brush the top and sides of the cake with apricot jam, then cover with marzipan (see page 13). Leave to dry. Attach the cake to a cake board with a little icing.

Flat-ice the top of the cake only with half the royal icing, giving it 2 coats (see page 13). Leave to dry. Thicken the rest of the icing with extra icing sugar, then use most of it to rough-ice the sides of the cake, pulling the icing up into peaks with a palette knife.

Tint one quarter of the moulding icing green and shape into 14 holly leaves (see page 53). Reserve the trimmings. Colour a little of the remaining moulding icing red and make some small berries, reserving the remainder. Leave the holly and berries to dry.

Shape some of the uncoloured moulding icing into 2 balls, for the head and body of the snowman. Press them gently together. Make a hat with the remaining red icing, and place on the head. Tint a little of the uncoloured moulding icing orange. Make 3 thin ropes of red, green and orange icing and twist them together to form a scarf, snipping the ends with scissors for tassels. Wrap around the snowman. Make a nose with a small piece of orange icing and three buttons with red icing. Colour a little of the uncoloured icing brown and shape a broomstick and eyes.

Place the snowman with the broomstick in centre of cake and make snowballs with the remaining uncoloured icing. Place the snowballs on top of the cake in piles around the snowman and arrange groups of holly leaves and berries around the top of the cake. Dust the snowman with a little icing sugar, for snow. Leave to set completely.

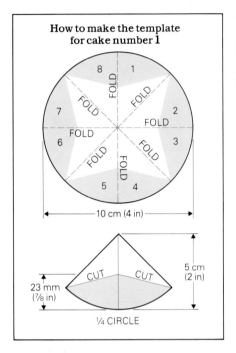

How to make the template
for cake number 1

10 cm (4 in)

5 cm
(2 in)

23 mm
(⅞ in)

CUT   CUT

¼ CIRCLE

Miniature Christmas cakes

These cakes make wonderful presents for those living alone, or to add to a Christmas hamper.

MAKES 4 × 10 cm (4 inch) CAKES

1 × 20 cm (8 inch) round tin Christmas cake mixture (see page 10 or 49)

For the decoration
4 tbls apricot jam, warmed and sieved
750 g (1½ lb) marzipan
4 × 18 cm (7 inch) round silver cake boards
royal icing made with 750 g (1½ lb) icing sugar (see page 13)
½ quantity moulding icing (see page 12)
silver dragees
Christmas roses (see page 52)
holly leaves and berries (see page 53)
red, yellow and green food colourings
1 metre (1 yard) Christmas ribbon

Heat the oven to 140°C, 275°F, Gas Mark 1.

To make the individual cake cases, cut out 4 × 25 cm (10 inch) circles of double thickness foil and mould each around the base and sides of an 850 g (1 lb 14 oz) can to make a 10 cm (4 inch) case. Remove the can carefully and place the cake cases on a baking sheet covered with double thickness brown paper.

Divide the cake mixture evenly among the foil cases and smooth the tops. Bake the cakes in the oven for 1¾-2 hours. Remove from the oven and allow to cool slightly, then remove the foil and leave to cool completely.

Brush the tops and sides of the cakes with jam, then cover with marzipan (see page 13), reserving the trimmings. Leave to dry. Attach the cakes to the cake boards with a little icing.

● Miniature Christmas cakes

Cake 1: Flat-ice the top of the cake with royal icing and allow to dry a little (see p.13). Then rough-ice sides, swirling into peaks with palette knife.

Make a template to fit the top of the cake. Fold into 8 and cut off a diagonal piece to form a star shape (see diagram). Mark the design on the cake, using a pin. Fill a greaseproof paper piping bag fitted with a star nozzle with royal icing. Pipe along the outline of the star. Press a silver dragee into each point of the star. Pipe around the top and base of the cake and place a Christmas rose in the centre.

Cake 2: Rough-ice all over with royal icing (see p.13). Decorate with holly leaves and berries (see p. 53).

Cake 3: Cover the cake with moulding

icing (see p.12) and reserve the trimmings to make the decorations. Using a plain nozzle and royal icing already in the piping bag, pipe 'Merry Christmas' across the top. Colour a little icing red and overpipe letters. Decorate with holly leaves and berries. Tie ribbon round.

Cake 4: Cover cake with moulding icing and reserve trimmings for decorations. Decorate with red candle shape with flame and holly. Tie ribbon round.

To make decorations divide reserved trimmings into 4 pieces. Keep 1 white and colour the other 3 red, green and yellow. Use white for Christmas rose; red for candle and holly berries, green for leaves (see pp.52-3) and yellow for candle flame.

HOW TO MAKE CHRISTMAS ROSES

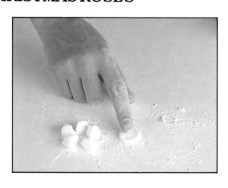

1 Lightly dust a work surface with icing sugar. Divide a small piece of untinted moulding icing into 6 equal pieces, to make the petals.

2 Shape one piece of the untinted moulding icing into a flat circle to use as a base for attaching the petals to the cake.

3 Shape the remaining 5 pieces of the moulding icing into flat petal shapes, slightly thinner than the base of the Christmas rose.

4 Arrange the petals overlapping slightly round the base. Press gently at the centre to make sure the petals adhere firmly.

5 Holding the outer edge of each petal at its centre pinch and press the petals to shape.

6 Tint moulding icing yellow and use to make 6 beads. Place 5 in circle at centre of flower and place 1 in middle.

HOW TO MAKE HOLLY LEAVES

1 Draw a basic holly leaf shape on to a small piece of thin card. Cut out with sharp scissors, to make the template for the leaves.

2 Colour some moulding icing a deep green, kneading the food colouring in thoroughly so that the icing is evenly tinted all the way through.

3 Roll out the icing on a board sprinkled with icing sugar, using a rolling pin dusted with icing sugar, to prevent the icing from sticking.

4 Place the template on the icing. Using a sharp knife, cut out the leaf, cutting right through the icing to give a neat outline.

5 Mark light indentations on the leaf with the tip of the knife, to represent the veins.

6 Mould the leaf into shape and bend into a slight curve. Rest over pencil to dry. Make berries from red-tinted icing.

Christening cake

If you wish to make the cake well ahead of the event, yellow or green colouring would be a good choice. Traditionalists might prefer to colour the cake blue for a boy or pink for a girl.

20 cm (8 inch) round rich fruit cake (see page 10)

For the icing and decoration
5 tbls apricot jam, warmed and sieved
500 g (1¼ lb) marzipan
1 quantity royal icing (see page 13)
1 quantity moulding icing (see page 12)
yellow food colouring
1 metre (1 yard) yellow ribbon
1 metre (1 yard) white fancy ribbon

Brush the top and sides of the cake with jam, then cover with marzipan (see page 13). Leave to dry. Fix to a silver cake board with a little royal icing.

Roll out the moulding icing and use to cover the cake (see page 12). Reserve the trimmings to make the cradle (see steps). Cut the ribbon to fit around the cake and secure it in place with a little royal icing.

Using a saucer or teaplate mark a 7.5 cm (3 inch) deep arc across one side of the cake. Mark 7 equally spaced lines radiating from the arc to the outer edge of the cake.

Half fill a greaseproof paper piping bag fitted with a star nozzle with royal icing. Pipe a double row of stars around the base of cake leaving a space between each star. Pipe a double row of stars a little apart around the top of the cake and pipe single rows of spaced stars along the marked design on the top.

Tint the remaining royal icing yellow and place in a piping bag fitted with a clean star nozzle. Pipe in between the white stars with yellow icing.

Place the cradle (see steps) within the iced arc and secure with a little icing.

How to make a moulded cradle

1 Place template pieces on to rolled out cornfloured moulding icing and cut around sides with a sharp knife. Make baby and rockers with trimmings.

2 Tint some icing yellow. Cut out pillow and quilt cover shapes. Score lightly with lattice pattern.

3 Pipe a thin line of royal icing around corners and base edges of cot pieces and assemble, starting with headboard and base.

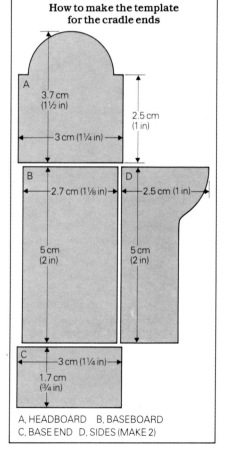

How to make the template for the cradle ends

A
3.7 cm (1½ in)
3 cm (1¼ in)
2.5 cm (1 in)

B
2.7 cm (1⅛ in)
5 cm (2 in)

D
2.5 cm (1 in)
5 cm (2 in)

C
3 cm (1¼ in)
1.7 cm (¾ in)

A, HEADBOARD   B, BASEBOARD
C, BASE END   D, SIDES (MAKE 2)

4 Leave to dry. Secure rockers to base with a little royal icing. Pipe small beads of yellow icing around edges.

Hearts and flowers wedding cake

15 cm (6 inch) round rich fruit cake
20 cm (8 inch) round rich fruit cake
25 cm (10 inch) round rich fruit cake
(see page 10 for recipes)

For the icing and decoration
*225 g (8 oz) apricot jam, warmed and
  sieved*
1.75 kg (4 lb) marzipan
*royal icing made with 2.75 kg (6 lb)
  icing sugar (see page 13)*
*20 cm (8 inch), 25 cm (10 inch) and
  30 cm (12 inch) round silver cake
  boards*
18 pink run-out hearts (see page 58)
red food colouring
18 piped pink roses (see page 63)
8 cake pillars
fresh roses

Brush the tops and sides of the cakes with jam, then cover with marzipan (see page 13). Leave to dry completely. Attach the cakes to the cake boards with a little royal icing.

Flat-ice the cakes with royal icing, giving 3 coats all over and a fourth coat to the top if necessary (see page 13). Leave to dry for 24 hours.

Make templates for the tops of the cakes. Fold each paper circle into 6 points and draw a curve from the rounded edge with a pencil. Cut the line with scissors, then open out. Transfer the design to cards.

Place the cards on top of the cakes and mark the design by pricking all round with a pin.

Using a greaseproof paper piping bag fitted with a plain nozzle, pipe a diagonal trellis design within the marked scallops. Using a star nozzle, pipe a row of stars on the outer edges of the cakes and around the bases. Attach 6 hearts to the side of each cake, spacing them below the centre of each scallop. Pipe a straight line of stars around the centre sides of each cake.

Tint a little icing pink and place in a piping bag fitted with a plain nozzle.

Pipe a looped design between every alternate star around sides of each cake. Secure the roses to the top of the cakes at the point of each scallop.

Asemble the cake tiers using 4 pillars on each tier and decorate the top of the cake with an arrangement of fresh roses to match the icing.

How to make a paper template for hearts and flowers wedding cake

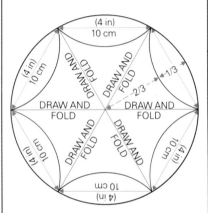

1 Group together the cake tins used to make the wedding cake. Using a soft pencil, draw round the base of each tin on to a sheet of greaseproof paper. Using sharp scissors, carefully cut out circles along pencil line.
2 Fold each circle in half. Using a ruler, mark the centre point in pencil on the fold (for a 20 cm/8 inch cake, mark centre point at 10 cm (4 inches). Then measure 10 cm (4 inches) from one end of fold line along to outer edge of circle and mark another point in pencil. From this point measure another 10 cm (4 inches) along outer edge of circle and mark another point. Repeat process on other half of circle.
3 Using a ruler, join outer points exactly through centre point, marking the lines in pencil. Then fold circle in half along pencil lines, always folding through centre point. This will give a circle divided into sixths. Using a saucer or a small tea plate, draw a curve into the circle area, no further in than one-third of the way to the centre point of the circle.

● Hearts and flowers wedding cake

HOW TO MAKE RUN-OUT HEARTS

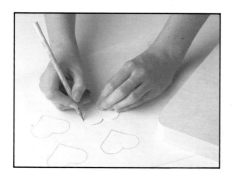

1 Draw a 4 cm (1½ inch) heart shape and trace to number required (allow extra) on underside of waxed or non-stick paper. Place on a board.

2 Tint icing, of piping consistency, pale pink. Place a little icing in a greaseproof paper piping bag fitted with a plain nozzle.

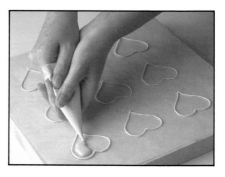

3 Pipe around the outline of the heart design, making sure there are no breaks and that the corners are closed.

4 Make a little icing thinner with egg white or lemon juice. Place in piping bag without nozzle. Snip point off bag and fill in design completely.

5 Use a cocktail stick to ease the icing into the corners. The icing should be level and slightly raised from the edges.

6 Leave to dry for 2-3 days. Peel off paper. Layer with tissue and store in airtight container.

Lacy wedding cake

This two-tier wedding cake makes an excellent alternative to the more traditional three-tier cake on pages 56 and 57. It is less costly in terms of ingredients, and less expert cake-makers will find the icing easier to accomplish. The template is not complicated, and once you have pricked out and defined the central area with iced lines (see diagram on page 60), then the rest of the outside area can be 'scribble' iced to give you a lace pattern. To do this, fit a thin writing nozzle to your piping bag, and 'scribble' at random without overlapping the icing line at any point. (As with all piping, it is best to practise on a plate first.)

Another point to bear in mind is that the floral arrangement on top of the cake should be attractive from all four sides, and should not be too high.

See recipe overleaf

Lacy wedding cake

20 cm (8 inch) square rich fruit cake
28 cm (11 inch) square rich fruit cake
(see page 10 for recipes)

For the icing and decoration
*225 g (8 oz) apricot jam, warmed and
   sieved*
2.5 kg (5½ lb) marzipan
*royal icing made with 2.75 kg (6 lb)
   icing sugar*
*25 cm (10 inch) and 33 cm (13 inch)
   square silver cake boards*
16 silver horseshoes
4 cake pillars
small vase with white flowers
*4 metres (3 yards) pale blue ribbon
   4 cm (1½ inches) wide*

Brush the tops and sides of the cake
with apricot jam, then cover with marzipan (see 13). Leave to dry completely.
Attach the cakes to the cake boards
with a little royal icing.

Flat-ice the cakes with royal icing,
giving 3 coats all over and a fourth coat
to the top if necessary (see page 13).
Leave to dry for 24 hours.

Make templates for the tops of the
cakes. Fold each square of paper diagonally to form a smaller triangle. Mark a
shallow 'V' from the long side of each
triangle, as in the diagram below. Cut
as indicated, then open out. Transfer
the design to cards.

Place the cards on top of each cake
and mark the design by pricking all
round with a pin.

Using a greaseproof paper piping bag
fitted with a medium plain nozzle, pipe
a line of royal icing around the marked
lines on the top of the cakes. Pipe a
second line of icing inside the first.
Overpipe a second line of icing on each
line using a smaller nozzle.

Using a thick plain nozzle, pipe a row
of dots around the top edges and base of
each cake and around the edge and
corners of each board. Work a lace pattern between the triangular outlines of
icing on each cake, taking it carefully
over the edges of the cakes. Pipe a simi-
lar pattern between the dotted outlines
on each board. Leave to dry. Attach
horseshoes to the top and bottom
corners of each cake.

Assemble the cake tiers using the
four pillars and decorate the top of the
cake with an arrangement of flowers in
a small vase. Attach the ribbon around
the sides of each cake and around the
vase at the top.

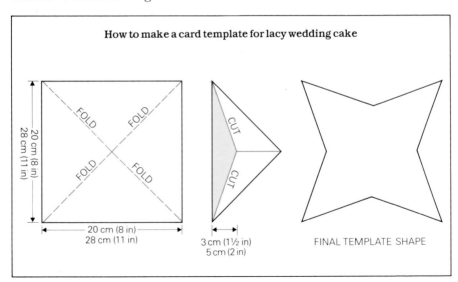

How to make a card template for lacy wedding cake

20 cm (8 in)
28 cm (11 in)

FOLD   FOLD
FOLD   FOLD

20 cm (8 in)
28 cm (11 in)

CUT
CUT

3 cm (1½ in)
5 cm (2 in)

FINAL TEMPLATE SHAPE

Good luck cake

This is a useful and stylish cake to have in your repertoire, as it is perfect for so many different occasions: a retirement party, friends emigrating, a new job or a change of career, an important exam, or a new school term.

If you wish to make a lighter cake use a sponge rather than a fruit cake mixture, and ice with either moulding or butter icing, and use bought cake decorations to finish. Remember this cake will need to be eaten sooner than an iced fruit cake.

If you can't find a horseshoe cake tin, improvise by baking the cake in a large round tin. Make two three-inch cuts into the cake at four and seven o'clock. Cut out a complete circle from the inner part of the cake, using the two initial cuts as a guide to the outside of this circle, then remove the wedge of cake between the two cuts.

See recipe overleaf

Good luck cake

25 cm (10 inch) round quantity rich fruit cake mixture, baked in a 25 cm (10 inch) horseshoe cake tin (see page 10).

For the icing and decoration
6 tbls apricot jam, warmed and sieved
1 kg (2 lb) marzipan
royal icing, made with 1.75 kg (4 lb)
icing sugar (see page 13)
33 cm (13 inch) round silver cake
board
Decoration
about 50 piped yellow roses (see
below and steps)
24 small silver leaves

Brush the top and sides of the cake with jam, then cover with marzipan (see page 13). Leave to dry completely. Attach the cake to a silver cake board with a little royal icing.

Flat-ice the cake with royal icing, giving 2 coats all over and a third coat to the top, if necessary (see page 13). Leave to dry for 24 hours. Cover the cake board with a little icing and attach the cake.

Using a star nozzle, pipe a coil around the top edges and around the base and ends of the horseshoe.

Using a little royal icing, attach 5 clusters of 3 roses and 2 silver leaves to the top of the cake at evenly spaced intervals. Attach pairs of roses and leaves to the sides of the cake, spacing around the outside, and 3 clusters around the inside and 1 on each end. Leave to set completely.

As well as the flowers you can make your own horseshoe decorations for this cake, with royal icing. Make small horseshoe templates of different sizes. Cut out the icing shapes and pipe a small scroll around the edges in a contrasting colour.

If you want to pipe 'good luck' on top of the cake trace out the lettering on a greaseproof paper template and prick out the lettering on to the iced surface of the cake.

Alternatively make or pipe decorations appropriate to the field in which you are wishing someone good luck: such as books for exams, a new school or college, a house for people moving into one, and so on.

To make the roses
To make the roses you need an icing nail or cork impaled on a skewer, a quantity of non-stick silicone paper cut into 5 cm (2 inch) squares and a greaseproof paper piping bag fitted with a large, medium or fine petal nozzle. For most cakes, a medium nozzle is most suitable.

HOW TO MAKE PIPED ROSES

1 Half fill the bag with stiff royal icing. Fold down the edges of the bag to exclude any air and prevent bubbles.

2 Secure a square of paper to the icing nail with a dab of icing.

3 Hold the piping bag so that the thin end of the petal nozzle is uppermost. Squeezing evenly and twisting nail, pipe tight coil for centre of rose.

4 Continue to add petals, one at a time, piping the icing and twisting at the same time, taking each petal about three-quarters the way round flower.

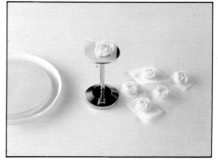

5 Pipe about 5 petals, beginning in a different part of the flower each time keeping base towards centre.

6 Leave the roses to dry for 24 hours before removing from the paper, then store in an airtight container.

INDEX